The Science of Prayer

Learning from the Master

Peter Gregory

Remnant Publications

Coldwater MI 49036
www.remnantpublications.com

Copyright © 2008
by Peter Gregory
All Rights Reserved
Printed in the USA

Published by
Remnant Publications
649 East Chicago Road
Coldwater MI 49036
517-279-1304
www.remnantpublications.com

Edited by Clifford Goldstein
Copy edited by Debi Tesser
Cover design by David Berthiaume
Text design by Greg Solie • AltamontGraphics.com

ISBN 978-1-933291-32-1

The Science of Prayer

"Our Father in heaven, hallowed be Your name. Your kingdom come. Your will be done on earth as it is in heaven. Give us this day our daily bread. And forgive us our debts, as we forgive our debtors. And do not lead us into temptation, but deliver us from the evil one. For Yours is the kingdom and the power and the glory forever. Amen" (Matthew 6:9–13, NKJV).

Are you, like me, frustrated sometimes by the way instructions are written? Though I have no problem buying goods from China, or from anywhere else in the world, I've learned that goods from China come with instructions that, at times, seem to have been written in

China, too, if you know what I mean? Bad instructions, or poorly written ones, can be worse than none at all!

When we want to do something, and do it right, if we don't know how to do it, then how crucial it is to get the proper instructions? And if it's that way with, for instance, the new computer you are trying to get up and running, or the new muffler you want to put on your car—then how much more so in the Christian life?

Of all the things in the Christian life, one of the most important is prayer, is it not? Indeed, we are told to pray. Jesus tells us to pray. Paul tells us to pray.

Yet, the question is, *"How do we pray? And do it correctly?*

This booklet is about the science of prayer—about how to pray. Most folks don't think of prayer as a science, and yet, in the sense that there is a method, a way to do it right—it is a science.

How, then, should we pray? What constitutes a good prayer? Is a longer prayer better than a short one, or is a short one better than a long one, or does it matter? Should we scream and shout in prayer, or should it be silent, from the heart alone?

The good news is that Jesus Himself gave us an example of how to pray. That is, we have instructions from the Master Himself. Thus, we can never say that we haven't been shown how.

Being Perfect

As we begin, the first thing we need to examine is the context in which this all arises. In Matthew 5:48, Jesus said, "Be ye therefore perfect, even as your Father which is in heaven is perfect." Many personal opinions exist about the words "perfect" or "perfection." But notice the word "therefore" in the text, indicating that what Jesus said here is a conclusion to what He already discussed in previous verses.

Look at what comes before, in verse 44, "But I say unto you, Love your enemies, bless them that curse you, do good to them that hate you, and pray for them which despitefully use you, and persecute you."

In other words, if you can love those who persecute you, who despitefully use you, and curse you—if you can love them, bless them, and pray for them—then you are on the way to being "perfect" as our Father in heaven is perfect. That's the kind of perfection exemplified here: character perfection, becoming like God, copying His image of perfect love.

"Be ye perfect," means that we need to know how to love our enemies the way that God loves everyone in this world. Even the most wicked person, even for the most evil and sinful person, God still loves them. In a similar way, we need to love them as well.

At the end of Matthew 5, we recognize our need to acquire Christ's perfection in character. So how do we love our enemies? What are the practical ways that we can learn how to love everyone as God loves them?

Learning from the Master

Not Being Hypocrites

Chapter 6 begins with this verse, "Take heed that ye do not your alms or good deeds before men, to be seen of them: otherwise ye have no reward of your Father which is in heaven." Thus, right after Jesus said, "Be ye perfect," He started to talk about us not showing off, not going around parading our piety and holiness before others. There's a connection here. Part obtaining a Christ-like character is not to display our good deeds ostentatiously.

Jesus continued, "Therefore when thou doest alms, do not sound a trumpet before thee, as the hypocrites do in the synagogues and in the streets, that they may have glory of men. Verily I say unto you, they have their reward. But when thou doest alms, let not thy left hand know what thy right hand doeth: that thy alms may be in secret: and thy Father which seeth in secret himself shall reward thee openly" (Matthew 6:2–4).

What Jesus meant was that God wants us to live an "invisible" Christian life. That's our duty. We need to somehow live a good Christian life "secretly." Yet, as we become invisible, God Himself will make us visible. God makes us open and known to other people; God makes us visible to other men. He promised to do it—not us.

Verse five reads, "And when thou prayest, thou shalt not be as the hypocrites are: for they love to pray standing in the synagogues and in the corners of the streets, that they may be seen of men. Verily I say unto you, they have their reward."

Jesus said that when we do good works, don't do them before men, don't do it in order to show your good works to others. That is not what prayer is ever to be. When we pray, we shouldn't do it to demonstrate how pious we want others to think that we are.

Some people, including myself, have not prayed day after day. So what do we do? When asked to pray in church, we make adjustments for what we didn't do in private, and so we pray long prayers, so long that when you end people utter "Amen!"—not

Learning from the Master

because of what you prayed but because the prayer has finally ended!

In Matthew 6:6, Jesus counseled how we should and should not pray, "But thou, when thou prayest, enter into thy closet, and when thou hast shut thy door, pray to thy Father which is in secret; and thy Father which seeth in secret shall reward thee openly."

So, when you do good things, do them as secretly as possible. When you pray, do it secretly as possible. This does not mean we cannot pray in a public setting, such as restaurants and the like. It means not to make a show of our prayers when we do pray in public places, not to try and prove our piety because that's not what a display of piety, holiness, or perfection should be.

We can see the link between being perfect and prayer: praying, and how we pray, leads to the kind of perfection of which Jesus spoke. Hence, how important it is that we learn to pray correctly!

Praying to the Wall

Let us learn from Jesus the characteristics of a prayer of merit, for this is key to the path of Christian perfection.

To begin, how should we pray so that we will be spiritually enriched? After all, who hasn't experienced, at times, a sense of deadness in their prayer lives? You just pray but don't sense any spiritual connection at all? You feel like you've been doing nothing but talking to the wall. I can't believe anyone hasn't felt that at some point or another.

Jesus continued. In Matthew 6:7, He says: "But when ye pray, use not vain repetitions as the heathen do: for they think that they shall be heard for their much speaking."

What does the Bible say regarding why the heathen pray with much repetition in chant-like prayers or for personal gain? It is because they want to be heard. So, from the Bible, what is the heathen attitude toward God? How do they understand their god? That god cannot hear, or he does not want to hear what they are saying. Why else would they feel the need to pray the same thing over, and over, and over again? If their god heard them the first time, that wouldn't be necessary, would it?

What may seem like a paradox, we also have scriptural counsel to repeat prayers as well. In Daniel 10, for example, Daniel prayed for three weeks to receive the understanding of a vision. We later learn that Michael waged a battle with Satan before he could carry the vision's meaning to Daniel. At Mt. Carmel, Elijah prayed seven times before the fire devoured the offering, altar, water, and everything that Elijah had offered to the Lord. In this case it was a test of faith. So a conclusion may be drawn that repetitive prayers that do not really say anything and just drone a sound, are not worth repeating. However, repetitive prayers that are prayed to strengthen faith and implore wisdom from the Lord are, indeed, worthy prayers.

Do we ever pray as though God does not want to hear us? There have been times when

I have felt as though God did not want to listen to me. But, based upon the Bible, when you go to God, if you are tempted to think that God does not want to hear you, you better just push away that thought because it's just not true. Everything we know about God should tell us that He wants to hear everything we have to say to Him. In fact, I would guess that He wants to hear considerably more from us than He already does.

In Japan, I visited a Shinto shrine, and before the holy place there was a big box, a box with a grill, and the worshipers would put their hands together, genuflect, and then throw money into the chest. They did not just put the money into the chest; instead, they actually threw it into the chest. I asked my Japanese interpreter, "Why do they throw their money into the chest like that?"

I don't know if he was joking, but he said, "They do it so that god can hear the money hitting the chest."

What does that mean? You have to awaken your god with your money? Listen to my prayer, because here it comes—100 yen worth. Following this logic to its conclusion, could we not say then that the more money we throw into the coffers, the louder it clinks in the chest, so the more likely God is to hear what we are saying?

God is not like that. No, God is ready to listen, even to anything that sounds like prayer. Even if you didn't say, "My Father which art in heaven … Amen," and even though you didn't have the nice, formal setting; even if you just sputter, "Oh, Lord, I need help;" God is always ready to listen. We don't have to awaken our God with money.

Our Father

In verse eight, Jesus continues, "Be not ye therefore like unto them: for your Father knoweth what things ye have need of, before ye ask him."

So why do we ask Him? Why do we pray to God? It's for our sake. Prayer doesn't change God; God is always the same. We pray because we need to be changed.

Yet, here is the kind of prayer that will transform our lives. Jesus shows us Himself how we are to pray. He says explicitly, "In this manner, therefore, pray" (Matthew 6:9, NKJV). How much clearer could He be? If you want to be "perfect," if you want to be changed, if you want to be all that you can be in the Lord, you need to learn how to pray. And Jesus shows us how!

"Our Father in heaven, hallowed be Your name. Your kingdom come. Your will be done on earth as it is in heaven. Give us this day our daily bread. And forgive us our debts, as we forgive our debtors. And do not lead us into temptation, but deliver us from the evil one. For Yours is the kingdom and the power and the glory forever. Amen" (Matthew 6:9–13, NKJV).

Let's look at these instructions as carefully as we can, for here we can find many powerful keys to demonstrate how to live the kind of Christian life that we all want to live. In this prayer, we have the best possible instructions on how to pray. We need to listen, too, because even the best instructions are useless if we don't follow them.

"After this manner therefore pray ye" (Matthew 6:9). Jesus didn't tell us to pray this rote prayer ever time we pray. Instead, He gave us this model, a form to emulate and to use as a foundational prayer. He imparted to us an outline of principles that, if followed, will change us, will mold us into the prayerful servants God wants us to be.

How, then, does the prayer itself begin? In the English Bible it begins with what word? "Our." But I believe the focus is on the next word: "Father."

The prayer needs to begin with what? With the Father, our Father, your Father. When we approach God, we must recognize that He is our Father. Sometimes we feel guilty that we haven't prayed for a long time, and so we rush through some lame prayer, and it's like, OK, we've done our religious duty, and then we walk away. Who hasn't been there and done that?

How much better to sit down before praying and have a little meditation and ask, "To whom am I praying? I'm praying to my Father—a loving, caring, heavenly Father who loved me so much that He sent His Son to die for me, to cover my sins, to grant me forgiveness, to give me the hope and promise of eternal life—a promise that I do not deserve. That's who my Father is, and He is the One to whom I pray."

The Bible says "Our Father." Notice with me that this whole prayer has a vertical and a horizontal experience—Father (vertical); our (horizontal)—it's not "my Father, give me daily bread, forgive me my trespasses, deliver me from. ..." No, we should always prayer, "*Our* Father ... deliver us."

What does this mean? Why is this important? What I believe Jesus is saying is that your prayer will be more meaningful if you pray not only for yourself but also for others.

Have you ever discovered the percentage of your prayer that is for yourself only? You pray in such a way that it seems as if everyone else can go to hell except you. We need to learn to pray for other people, according to the example of Jesus.

So look at this prayer very carefully. It says, "Our Father which art in heaven, hallowed be Thy name. Thy kingdom come, thy will be done on earth as it is in heaven."

It first points us to the Father in heaven. After that, the prayer states, "Give us this day our daily bread." In other words, when you have recognized who God is, where He is, and the purpose of God, when you're connected with Him—then you can pray about your needs. That's the example from Jesus.

Prayer and Obedience

This prayer is also tied directly to obedience to God. What do I mean? "Our Father," that means our God is our Father. The first commandment says that "Thou shalt have no other gods before Me" (Exodus 20:3) because our God is Father. It then says "which art in heaven," and the Bible says, "No man hath seen God" (1 John 4:12). We have not seen Him He is in heaven, and because of that the second commandment says, "Thou shalt not make unto thee any graven image …" (Exodus 20:4).

"Hallowed be Thy name." The third commandment reads, "Thou shalt not take the name of the Lord Thy God in vain" (Exodus 20:7).

The prayer says too, "Thy kingdom come. Thy will be done in earth, as it is in heaven." That has so much meaning behind it. God's will be done on earth. It says, "Your kingdom can come when Your will is done on earth." God's will on earth in the last days will be centered around obedience to the fourth commandment, the Sabbath.[1]

Continuing, the prayer says, "Give us this day our daily bread. And forgive us our debts, as we forgive our debtors." And then it says, "Lead us not into temptation,

---

[1] For further discussion on the Sabbath message, please see *A Day to Remember*, by Dwight Hall, Remnant Publications, Coldwater, MI.

but deliver us from evil." Those two phrases deal with the last six commandments (Exodus 20:12–17).

What are the temptations we face every day? Dishonoring our parents, hatred, lust, stealing, lying, covetousness—these are the temptations. So the Lord's Prayer, if we pray in a true and sincere way, will help us keep God's Ten Commandments.

A Sanctified Life

"Our Father which art in heaven, hallowed be Thy name." After recognizing that He is our Father, we must hallow His name. When was the first time the Bible used a word that means "hallowed" in the Bible? Genesis 2—and what was hallowed? The Sabbath. "Hallowed" means sacred, sanctified, set apart, holy. So when we say, "Hallowed be Thy name," it's not like we can make God's name more holy than it is. When we pray "Hallowed be Thy name," we are really praying "May the name of God be sanctified in my life."

What does that mean, the name of our Father being sanctified in our life? What is the name of God according to the Bible? There are many answers and many names, but there is only one that fits this purpose. Remember when Moses asked the Father, "Show me Thy glory" (Exodus 3:18)? God responded, "I will pass all my goodness before thee and I will proclaim the name of the LORD before thee." So God's name is equal to God's glory. Follow by these words, "and will be gracious to whom I will be gracious, and will show mercy on whom I will show mercy" (Exodus 33:19).

When we talk about the name of God, in this sense, what is the characteristic of God's name? It is His glory, His character, His goodness, His mercy, His grace. That name, then, needs to be exhibited in our lives. When we pray "Hallowed be Thy name," it reveals that God's name is, somehow, manifested in our lives. It is believing that His character, His authority, His honor, all that He possesses, and

Learning from the Master

is, can be used to help us live His life in this world.

We don't pray like this often, do we? Instead, many times we talk to God, not even really thinking with whom we're speaking; we don't recognize who He is. We're just concerned about, "Please Lord, take away my sins, just take care of me. I feel bad; make me feel good. I am so poor; make me rich. I have an exam today; please help me to pass the test." We're so concerned about our needs so many times we pray only about ourselves; even worse, we don't think about who God really is when we pray to Him.

Because we didn't recognize who God is when we pray, we then walk away from your prayer as though we do not believe that what we prayed will come to pass. Isn't that so often true? Why? Because in a sense, we have prayed to ourselves and not to God.

Look at this powerful verse. It says it all, "But without faith it is impossible to please him: for he that cometh to God must believe that He is" God (Hebrews 11:6). You know what that means? Many people who will pray to God, but they do not believe that He is God; they do not recognize that He is the Father; He is holy and sacred, and He exists in heaven! They pray like the pagans; they pray like the heathen—they care only about themselves.

How important, then, that we take the time to recognize just who "Our Father in heaven" really is, what He had done for us, and what He promises us. We who beseech God must believe that He is God; we must believe that He is who He says He is, and that He will do for us what He promises He will do.

Without that, in a sense, we might as well be praying to the wall.

Prayer and Prophecy

"Thy kingdom come." What does that mean?

There is the kingdom of grace, under which we now live, and kingdom of glory, in which we will live. Of course this kingdom also means a kingdom of grace, but, ultimately, this is means the kingdom of glory—the second coming of Christ. On an interesting note, Jesus wanted us to remember the second coming when we pray.

That really shouldn't be surprising, should it? After all, think about it. What is our greatest hope, what is the greatest promise we have, if not the second coming of Jesus? Without it, without the resurrection of the dead, without the transformation of the living into incorruptible bodies, what does our religion mean? Nothing, really. Without it, we live; we suffer; we die forever. What good will that do us, even if all our prayers in this life are answered now, if we don't have the eternal life in a new heaven and a new earth that we have been promised? No good at all! No wonder Jesus, with this model prayer, points us to the promise of His second coming.

"Thy Kingdom come." How many of us pray that God's kingdom will come? Or are we afraid that His coming will be too soon—you know, before we get married, before we graduate, before we get fancy new car? Are you afraid that Jesus will come too soon?

When we realize who He is, where He is, and what kind of God He is, you will say, "I want my Father to return! I want my heavenly Father to return; I want my Holy Father's kingdom to come—Thy kingdom come!"

But look at the context in which this appears. Thy kingdom come and "Thy will be done on earth." Until the will of God is done on earth, He will not return. In other words, it seems to be saying that only when His will has been completed on earth will He return.

Then, the crucial question naturally is—what is the will of God? Psalm 40:8 tells us: "I delight to do Thy will, O my God; yea, Thy law is within my heart."

The law of God, God's Ten Commandments, is His will. So the Ten Commandments must live in our hearts. Somehow the Ten Commandments must be kept in our hearts before Jesus can return and take us home.

Look at the text more fully: "Thy will be done on earth, as it is in heaven." What does that mean? It means that the will of God (the Ten Commandments) needs to be kept here on earth the way that the commandments are kept in heaven.

Who keeps the commandments of God in heaven? The angels, who else? How do the angels keep God's commandments? Though we aren't told, they certainly do it with an attitude of praise, of thankfulness, of joy, don't you think? I would surmise that they say things like, "I'm glad to do this! I love to do this! I want to worship Him! I want to do His will! I truly love God and want to stay close to Him! This is my joy! I would never want to disobey the Lord, who loves us so much!"

What an attitude! Not like, "Oh, man, I've got to keep this and do that." "Alright, I guess I'll go to church today." "Oh … I guess I have to make things right." "Aw, I've got to restrict myself and do this thing or that no matter how much fun it would be." "Oh, no— this is such a heavy burden. I'll do it but what a drag, man!"

The angels in heaven do not know God's commandments that way. Perhaps some once did—the ones who fell with Lucifer.

Thus, we need to pray until our hearts change, until it becomes our joy to keep His commandments, until we delight to do the will of God, until we can pray, "Lord, Thy will be done on earth as it is in heaven. Help me to love to do Your will."

Our Daily Bread

Jesus' prayer instructions continued, "Give us this day our daily bread," This is asking God to fill our basic, temporal needs. But this means more than temporal food; this signifies about spiritual food as well, and true spiritual food, true spiritual bread, will transform us into His image. So we must pray until we can visualize that we are being transformed into the image

Learning from the Master

of God; we must believe that God is doing that in our minds. Every time we pray, it is like a mind operation, brain surgery, and that doesn't mean how long or how loud we pray; this means how we pray—for that really transforms our lives.

Imagine the life of Jesus, especially the closing scenes, the last hours of His earthly ministry, the hours that led to Calvary. "Watch" Him, the way He dealt with His enemies, with Judas, with Peter, with the Sanhedrin, with the Roman soldiers and the mob, the thief. Picture all of that and then reflect that character in your own life, when you come face to face with your own Judas, your own Peter, your own Sanhedrin, your own mob, and your own thief.

Pray, "Lord, help me to be like Jesus!" Embrace that prayer until it is seasoned in your wicked mind so that your wicked mind will be cleansed, so that when you get up from your prayer you still have the fragrance of Christ and His righteousness surrounding you.

This will never happen with just a quick, get-out-of-the-way prayer, your religious duty done for the day. That kind of prayer will never change us. That's just wasting our time; we would make better use of our time in studying for the next exam, or talking to friends on the phone, or instant messaging them, for that matter. That kind of prayer is an insult to God and can be very deceptive as well, for it makes you think you are living right when you are not. After all, I'm a Christian because I pray! It's not as simple as that.

"Give us this day our daily bread." Our spiritual food is a daily portion. You cannot live off yesterday's prayer. You cannot live today like, "I am not praying this week, but Sabbath is coming." When Sabbath comes, I will pray a lot. That should not be how we think about prayer.

When we are charged, when we are filled with His character and fully fueled, then we can pray, "Forgive our debts, as we forgive our debtors." We cannot practice any act of mercy on others unless we are healed with a spiritual healing. And when we have this forgiving spirit toward others, then we can pray, "Lead us not into temptation but deliver us from evil."

You know why we keep falling? While we fall for many reasons, I believe there's one in particular—we keep falling into temptation because we do not have a forgiving spirit. We hate somebody we harbor bitterness toward someone; we may hold a grudge against someone and will not release the anger, and when we hold onto that bitterness, it can poison our whole spiritual lives. Why? Because when you keep holding onto that bitterness, when you pray, you pray for everything in the world except for that person. Consequently, our spiritual lives will arrive at a dead end because of holding onto that bitter and unforgiving spirit, resentment, jealousy, or even hatred. We must let it go.

Thus, you need to pray, "Feed me spiritual food daily, and then I can have a forgiving spirit toward others." When I pray this way, it helps me to overcome temptations. It will work for you as well, I guarantee it.

Jesus shows us more, "But deliver us from evil: for thine is the kingdom, and the power, and glory, for ever. Amen."

We need to ask to be delivered from evil. If not, we will naturally gravitate toward it. That's what being a fallen creature means—having a natural inherent bent toward evil. Thus, without supernatural help, we will be delivered into evil when we need to be delivered from it. When we pray for deliverance from evil, focus not on the evil, but direct your mind to the Deliverer. So we pray to be reminded of the Deliverer, not so much the evil that might captivate us.

The bottom line? How is your prayer life? Attending church every Sabbath alone cannot help your spiritual life. I want to challenge you—to find a need a spot, a physical spot, a designated place, a meeting place with God; that place maybe a quiet park, maybe in your backyard, maybe that special room in your house; maybe in your car; maybe in your bedroom. But you have to designate one location where you alone can pour out your heart to the Lord.

Instructions

Jesus taught us the basics of prayer. We are told to pray, and we have looked at some of the instructions on how to do it. We've had the best Teacher the world has ever known teach us how to pray. But, as we said before, we can have the best instructions possible, but if we don't follow them, if we don't take them out of the box and read them and follow them, they'll do us no good at all.

Let's look at those instructions one last time. But more than that: Let's take them and follow them with all our hearts, souls, spirits, and minds. If so, our lives will never be the same again:

"Our Father in heaven, hallowed be Your name. Your kingdom come. Your will be done on earth as it is in heaven. Give us this day our daily bread. And forgive us our debts, as we forgive our debtors. And do not lead us into temptation, but deliver us from the evil one. For Yours is the kingdom and the power and the glory forever. Amen" (Matthew 6:9–13, NKJV).